||||| ||| | |||||| ||| |||||| ||| |||||| |||
I0053081

ADDRESS BOOK
QUAIL

The Pocket Size Address Book

All rights reserved. No part of this document may be reproduced or transmitted in any form or by any means, electronic or otherwise. This means that you cannot record or photocopy any material Ideas, tips or suggestions that are provided in this book

www.journalsrus.com

Address Book Quail
© 2016 Ciparum LLC
All rights reserved.
ISBN-10:1-63589-067-5
ISBN-13:978-1-63589-067-9

Table of Content

Name	Page		Name	Page

Name	Page		Name	Page

THIS PAGE WAS
INTENTIONALLY
LEFT BLANK

NAME..

ADDRESS..

....

MOBILE # (Cell)...

HOME #...

WORK #..

FAX...

EMAIL...

NAME..

ADDRESS..

....

MOBILE # (Cell)...

HOME #...

WORK #..

FAX...

EMAIL...

NAME..

ADDRESS..

....

MOBILE # (Cell)...

HOME #...

WORK #..

FAX...

EMAIL...

NOTES:

NAME..

ADDRESS..

....

MOBILE # (Cell)...

HOME #...

WORK #...

FAX...

EMAIL...

NAME..

ADDRESS..

....

MOBILE # (Cell)...

HOME #...

WORK #...

FAX...

EMAIL...

NAME..

ADDRESS..

....

MOBILE # (Cell)...

HOME #...

WORK #...

FAX...

EMAIL...

NOTES:

NAME..

ADDRESS...

....

MOBILE # (Cell)..

HOME #...

WORK #...

FAX...

EMAIL...

NAME..

ADDRESS...

....

MOBILE # (Cell)..

HOME #...

WORK #...

FAX...

EMAIL...

NAME..

ADDRESS...

....

MOBILE # (Cell)..

HOME #...

WORK #...

FAX...

EMAIL...

NOTES:

NAME...
ADDRESS...
....
MOBILE # (Cell)...
HOME #..
WORK #..
FAX...
EMAIL..

NAME...
ADDRESS...
....
MOBILE # (Cell)...
HOME #..
WORK #..
FAX...
EMAIL..

NAME...
ADDRESS...
....
MOBILE # (Cell)...
HOME #..
WORK #..
FAX...
EMAIL..

NOTES:

NAME..

ADDRESS...

....

MOBILE # (Cell)...

HOME #..

WORK #..

FAX..

EMAIL..

NAME..

ADDRESS...

....

MOBILE # (Cell)...

HOME #..

WORK #..

FAX..

EMAIL..

NAME..

ADDRESS...

....

MOBILE # (Cell)...

HOME #..

WORK #..

FAX..

EMAIL..

NOTES:

NAME...
ADDRESS...
....
MOBILE # (Cell)..
HOME #...
WORK #...
FAX..
EMAIL..

NAME...
ADDRESS...
....
MOBILE # (Cell)..
HOME #...
WORK #...
FAX..
EMAIL..

NAME...
ADDRESS...
....
MOBILE # (Cell)..
HOME #...
WORK #...
FAX..
EMAIL..

NOTES:

NAME...

ADDRESS..

....

MOBILE # (Cell)...

HOME #...

WORK #..

FAX..

EMAIL...

NAME...

ADDRESS..

....

MOBILE # (Cell)...

HOME #...

WORK #..

FAX..

EMAIL...

NAME...

ADDRESS..

....

MOBILE # (Cell)...

HOME #...

WORK #..

FAX..

EMAIL...

NOTES:

NAME..

ADDRESS...

....

MOBILE # (Cell)...

HOME #...

WORK #...

FAX...

EMAIL...

NAME..

ADDRESS...

....

MOBILE # (Cell)...

HOME #...

WORK #...

FAX...

EMAIL...

NAME..

ADDRESS...

....

MOBILE # (Cell)...

HOME #...

WORK #...

FAX...

EMAIL...

NOTES:

NAME...

ADDRESS..

....

MOBILE # (Cell)..

HOME #...

WORK #...

FAX..

EMAIL...

NAME...

ADDRESS..

....

MOBILE # (Cell)..

HOME #...

WORK #...

FAX..

EMAIL...

NAME...

ADDRESS..

....

MOBILE # (Cell)..

HOME #...

WORK #...

FAX..

EMAIL...

NOTES:

NAME..
ADDRESS...
....
MOBILE # (Cell)..
HOME #...
WORK #...
FAX..
EMAIL...

NAME..
ADDRESS...
....
MOBILE # (Cell)..
HOME #...
WORK #...
FAX..
EMAIL...

NAME..
ADDRESS...
....
MOBILE # (Cell)..
HOME #...
WORK #...
FAX..
EMAIL...

NOTES:

NAME...

ADDRESS...

....

MOBILE # (Cell)...

HOME #...

WORK #...

FAX..

EMAIL...

NAME...

ADDRESS...

....

MOBILE # (Cell)...

HOME #...

WORK #...

FAX..

EMAIL...

NAME...

ADDRESS...

....

MOBILE # (Cell)...

HOME #...

WORK #...

FAX..

EMAIL...

NOTES:

NAME...
ADDRESS...
....
MOBILE # (Cell)...
HOME #...
WORK #..
FAX...
EMAIL..

NAME...
ADDRESS...
....
MOBILE # (Cell)...
HOME #...
WORK #..
FAX...
EMAIL..

NAME...
ADDRESS...
....
MOBILE # (Cell)...
HOME #...
WORK #..
FAX...
EMAIL..

NOTES:

NAME...

ADDRESS..

....

MOBILE # (Cell)..

HOME #...

WORK #..

FAX..

EMAIL...

NAME...

ADDRESS..

....

MOBILE # (Cell)..

HOME #...

WORK #..

FAX..

EMAIL...

NAME...

ADDRESS..

....

MOBILE # (Cell)..

HOME #...

WORK #..

FAX..

EMAIL...

NOTES:

NAME..

ADDRESS..

....

MOBILE # (Cell)..

HOME #..

WORK #...

FAX...

EMAIL...

NAME..

ADDRESS..

....

MOBILE # (Cell)..

HOME #..

WORK #...

FAX...

EMAIL...

NAME..

ADDRESS..

....

MOBILE # (Cell)..

HOME #..

WORK #...

FAX...

EMAIL...

NOTES:

NAME..
ADDRESS..
....
MOBILE # (Cell)..
HOME #...
WORK #...
FAX...
EMAIL..

NAME..
ADDRESS..
....
MOBILE # (Cell)..
HOME #...
WORK #...
FAX...
EMAIL..

NAME..
ADDRESS..
....
MOBILE # (Cell)..
HOME #...
WORK #...
FAX...
EMAIL..

NOTES:

NAME..
ADDRESS...
....
MOBILE # (Cell)...
HOME #...
WORK #...
FAX...
EMAIL..

NAME..
ADDRESS...
....
MOBILE # (Cell)...
HOME #...
WORK #...
FAX...
EMAIL..

NAME..
ADDRESS...
....
MOBILE # (Cell)...
HOME #...
WORK #...
FAX...
EMAIL..

NOTES:

NAME..

ADDRESS..

....

MOBILE # (Cell)...

HOME #...

WORK #...

FAX...

EMAIL..

NAME..

ADDRESS..

....

MOBILE # (Cell)...

HOME #...

WORK #...

FAX...

EMAIL..

NAME..

ADDRESS..

....

MOBILE # (Cell)...

HOME #...

WORK #...

FAX...

EMAIL..

NOTES:

NAME..

ADDRESS...

....

MOBILE # (Cell)...

HOME #..

WORK #...

FAX..

EMAIL...

NAME..

ADDRESS...

....

MOBILE # (Cell)...

HOME #..

WORK #...

FAX..

EMAIL...

NAME..

ADDRESS...

....

MOBILE # (Cell)...

HOME #..

WORK #...

FAX..

EMAIL...

NOTES:

NAME...

ADDRESS...

....

MOBILE # (Cell)..

HOME #...

WORK #...

FAX..

EMAIL..

NAME...

ADDRESS...

....

MOBILE # (Cell)..

HOME #...

WORK #...

FAX..

EMAIL..

NAME...

ADDRESS...

....

MOBILE # (Cell)..

HOME #...

WORK #...

FAX..

EMAIL..

NOTES:

19

NAME..

ADDRESS...

....

MOBILE # (Cell)..

HOME #...

WORK #...

FAX...

EMAIL...

NAME..

ADDRESS...

....

MOBILE # (Cell)..

HOME #...

WORK #...

FAX...

EMAIL...

NAME..

ADDRESS...

....

MOBILE # (Cell)..

HOME #...

WORK #...

FAX...

EMAIL...

NOTES:

NAME..

ADDRESS...

....

MOBILE # (Cell)...

HOME #...

WORK #...

FAX...

EMAIL...

NAME..

ADDRESS...

....

MOBILE # (Cell)...

HOME #...

WORK #...

FAX...

EMAIL...

NAME..

ADDRESS...

....

MOBILE # (Cell)...

HOME #...

WORK #...

FAX...

EMAIL...

NOTES:

NAME...
ADDRESS...
....
MOBILE # (Cell)..
HOME #...
WORK #..
FAX..
EMAIL..

NAME...
ADDRESS...
....
MOBILE # (Cell)..
HOME #...
WORK #..
FAX..
EMAIL..

NAME...
ADDRESS...
....
MOBILE # (Cell)..
HOME #...
WORK #..
FAX..
EMAIL..

NOTES:

NAME..

ADDRESS..

....

MOBILE # (Cell)..

HOME #..

WORK #..

FAX...

EMAIL...

NAME..

ADDRESS..

....

MOBILE # (Cell)..

HOME #..

WORK #..

FAX...

EMAIL...

NAME..

ADDRESS..

....

MOBILE # (Cell)..

HOME #..

WORK #..

FAX...

EMAIL...

NOTES:

NAME..

ADDRESS..

....

MOBILE # (Cell)..

HOME #..

WORK #..

FAX..

EMAIL..

NAME..

ADDRESS..

....

MOBILE # (Cell)..

HOME #..

WORK #..

FAX..

EMAIL..

NAME..

ADDRESS..

....

MOBILE # (Cell)..

HOME #..

WORK #..

FAX..

EMAIL..

NOTES:

NAME...

ADDRESS...

....

MOBILE # (Cell)..

HOME #...

WORK #...

FAX...

EMAIL..

NAME...

ADDRESS...

....

MOBILE # (Cell)..

HOME #...

WORK #...

FAX...

EMAIL..

NAME...

ADDRESS...

....

MOBILE # (Cell)..

HOME #...

WORK #...

FAX...

EMAIL..

NOTES:

NAME..
ADDRESS..
....
MOBILE # (Cell)...
HOME #...
WORK #...
FAX...
EMAIL..

NAME..
ADDRESS..
....
MOBILE # (Cell)...
HOME #...
WORK #...
FAX...
EMAIL..

NAME..
ADDRESS..
....
MOBILE # (Cell)...
HOME #...
WORK #...
FAX...
EMAIL..

NOTES:

NAME..

ADDRESS..…...

....….

MOBILE # (Cell)..…..…..

HOME #...…..…...

WORK #...…........

FAX...…..

EMAIL...…..

NAME..

ADDRESS..…...

....….

MOBILE # (Cell)..…..…..

HOME #...…..…...

WORK #...…........

FAX...…..

EMAIL...…..

NAME..

ADDRESS..…...

....….

MOBILE # (Cell)..…..…..

HOME #...…..…...

WORK #...…........

FAX...…..

EMAIL...…..

NOTES:

NAME...

ADDRESS..

....

MOBILE # (Cell)..

HOME #...

WORK #..

FAX..

EMAIL..

NAME...

ADDRESS..

....

MOBILE # (Cell)..

HOME #...

WORK #..

FAX..

EMAIL..

NAME...

ADDRESS..

....

MOBILE # (Cell)..

HOME #...

WORK #..

FAX..

EMAIL..

NOTES:

NAME..

ADDRESS...

....

MOBILE # (Cell)..

HOME #...

WORK #...

FAX..

EMAIL...

NAME..

ADDRESS...

....

MOBILE # (Cell)..

HOME #...

WORK #...

FAX..

EMAIL...

NAME..

ADDRESS...

....

MOBILE # (Cell)..

HOME #...

WORK #...

FAX..

EMAIL...

NOTES:

NAME...
ADDRESS...
....
MOBILE # (Cell)...
HOME #..
WORK #...
FAX..
EMAIL...

___

NAME...
ADDRESS...
....
MOBILE # (Cell)...
HOME #..
WORK #...
FAX..
EMAIL...

___

NAME...
ADDRESS...
....
MOBILE # (Cell)...
HOME #..
WORK #...
FAX..
EMAIL...

___

NOTES:

NAME...

ADDRESS...

....

MOBILE # (Cell)..

HOME #...

WORK #...

FAX...

EMAIL..

NAME...

ADDRESS...

....

MOBILE # (Cell)..

HOME #...

WORK #...

FAX...

EMAIL..

NAME...

ADDRESS...

....

MOBILE # (Cell)..

HOME #...

WORK #...

FAX...

EMAIL..

NOTES:

NAME...

ADDRESS...

....

MOBILE # (Cell)...

HOME #...

WORK #...

FAX..

EMAIL..

NAME...

ADDRESS...

....

MOBILE # (Cell)...

HOME #...

WORK #...

FAX..

EMAIL..

NAME...

ADDRESS...

....

MOBILE # (Cell)...

HOME #...

WORK #...

FAX..

EMAIL..

NOTES:

NAME...

ADDRESS...

....

MOBILE # (Cell)...

HOME #...

WORK #...

FAX...

EMAIL..

NAME...

ADDRESS...

....

MOBILE # (Cell)...

HOME #...

WORK #...

FAX...

EMAIL..

NAME...

ADDRESS...

....

MOBILE # (Cell)...

HOME #...

WORK #...

FAX...

EMAIL..

NOTES:

NAME..

ADDRESS..

....

MOBILE # (Cell)..

HOME #...

WORK #...

FAX...

EMAIL..

NAME..

ADDRESS..

....

MOBILE # (Cell)..

HOME #...

WORK #...

FAX...

EMAIL..

NAME..

ADDRESS..

....

MOBILE # (Cell)..

HOME #...

WORK #...

FAX...

EMAIL..

NOTES:

NAME...

ADDRESS..

....

MOBILE # (Cell)...

HOME #...

WORK #..

FAX..

EMAIL...

NAME...

ADDRESS..

....

MOBILE # (Cell)...

HOME #...

WORK #..

FAX..

EMAIL...

NAME...

ADDRESS..

....

MOBILE # (Cell)...

HOME #...

WORK #..

FAX..

EMAIL...

NOTES:

NAME..

ADDRESS...

....

MOBILE # (Cell)...

HOME #..

WORK #..

FAX..

EMAIL...

NAME..

ADDRESS...

....

MOBILE # (Cell)...

HOME #..

WORK #..

FAX..

EMAIL...

NAME..

ADDRESS...

....

MOBILE # (Cell)...

HOME #..

WORK #..

FAX..

EMAIL...

NOTES:

NAME...
ADDRESS...
....
MOBILE # (Cell)..
HOME #..
WORK #..
FAX...
EMAIL...

NAME...
ADDRESS...
....
MOBILE # (Cell)..
HOME #..
WORK #..
FAX...
EMAIL...

NAME...
ADDRESS...
....
MOBILE # (Cell)..
HOME #..
WORK #..
FAX...
EMAIL...

NOTES:

NAME...

ADDRESS..

....

MOBILE # (Cell)..

HOME #...

WORK #...

FAX...

EMAIL...

NAME...

ADDRESS..

....

MOBILE # (Cell)..

HOME #...

WORK #...

FAX...

EMAIL...

NAME...

ADDRESS..

....

MOBILE # (Cell)..

HOME #...

WORK #...

FAX...

EMAIL...

NOTES:

NAME..
ADDRESS..
....
MOBILE # (Cell)...
HOME #...
WORK #...
FAX..
EMAIL..

NAME..
ADDRESS..
....
MOBILE # (Cell)...
HOME #...
WORK #...
FAX..
EMAIL..

NAME..
ADDRESS..
....
MOBILE # (Cell)...
HOME #...
WORK #...
FAX..
EMAIL..

NOTES:

NAME..

ADDRESS..

....

MOBILE # (Cell)..

HOME #..

WORK #..

FAX...

EMAIL...

NAME..

ADDRESS..

....

MOBILE # (Cell)..

HOME #..

WORK #..

FAX...

EMAIL...

NAME..

ADDRESS..

....

MOBILE # (Cell)..

HOME #..

WORK #..

FAX...

EMAIL...

NOTES:

NAME..

ADDRESS...

....

MOBILE # (Cell)...

HOME #...

WORK #...

FAX...

EMAIL..

NAME..

ADDRESS...

....

MOBILE # (Cell)...

HOME #...

WORK #...

FAX...

EMAIL..

NAME..

ADDRESS...

....

MOBILE # (Cell)...

HOME #...

WORK #...

FAX...

EMAIL..

NOTES:

NAME...
ADDRESS...
....
MOBILE # (Cell)..
HOME #..
WORK #..
FAX...
EMAIL..

NAME...
ADDRESS...
....
MOBILE # (Cell)..
HOME #..
WORK #..
FAX...
EMAIL..

NAME...
ADDRESS...
....
MOBILE # (Cell)..
HOME #..
WORK #..
FAX...
EMAIL..

NOTES:

NAME..
ADDRESS..
....
MOBILE # (Cell)...
HOME #...
WORK #...
FAX...
EMAIL..

NAME..
ADDRESS..
....
MOBILE # (Cell)...
HOME #...
WORK #...
FAX...
EMAIL..

NAME..
ADDRESS..
....
MOBILE # (Cell)...
HOME #...
WORK #...
FAX...
EMAIL..

NOTES:

NAME...
ADDRESS..
....
MOBILE # (Cell)..
HOME #...
WORK #...
FAX..
EMAIL..

NAME...
ADDRESS..
....
MOBILE # (Cell)..
HOME #...
WORK #...
FAX..
EMAIL..

NAME...
ADDRESS..
....
MOBILE # (Cell)..
HOME #...
WORK #...
FAX..
EMAIL..

NOTES:

NAME..
ADDRESS..
....
MOBILE # (Cell)..
HOME #..
WORK #..
FAX...
EMAIL..

NAME..
ADDRESS..
....
MOBILE # (Cell)..
HOME #..
WORK #..
FAX...
EMAIL..

NAME..
ADDRESS..
....
MOBILE # (Cell)..
HOME #..
WORK #..
FAX...
EMAIL..

NOTES:

NAME..
ADDRESS...
....
MOBILE # (Cell)...
HOME #..
WORK #..
FAX..
EMAIL...

NAME..
ADDRESS...
....
MOBILE # (Cell)...
HOME #..
WORK #..
FAX..
EMAIL...

NAME..
ADDRESS...
....
MOBILE # (Cell)...
HOME #..
WORK #..
FAX..
EMAIL...

NOTES:

NAME...
ADDRESS..
....
MOBILE # (Cell)..
HOME #...
WORK #...
FAX..
EMAIL..

NAME...
ADDRESS..
....
MOBILE # (Cell)..
HOME #...
WORK #...
FAX..
EMAIL..

NAME...
ADDRESS..
....
MOBILE # (Cell)..
HOME #...
WORK #...
FAX..
EMAIL..

NOTES:

NAME...
ADDRESS...
....
MOBILE # (Cell)..
HOME #...
WORK #...
FAX..
EMAIL...

NAME...
ADDRESS...
....
MOBILE # (Cell)..
HOME #...
WORK #...
FAX..
EMAIL...

NAME...
ADDRESS...
....
MOBILE # (Cell)..
HOME #...
WORK #...
FAX..
EMAIL...

NOTES:

NAME...
ADDRESS..
....
MOBILE # (Cell)...
HOME #...
WORK #...
FAX..
EMAIL...

NAME...
ADDRESS..
....
MOBILE # (Cell)...
HOME #...
WORK #...
FAX..
EMAIL...

NAME...
ADDRESS..
....
MOBILE # (Cell)...
HOME #...
WORK #...
FAX..
EMAIL...

NOTES:

NAME..

ADDRESS...

....

MOBILE # (Cell)...

HOME #...

WORK #...

FAX...

EMAIL..

NAME..

ADDRESS...

....

MOBILE # (Cell)...

HOME #...

WORK #...

FAX...

EMAIL..

NAME..

ADDRESS...

....

MOBILE # (Cell)...

HOME #...

WORK #...

FAX...

EMAIL..

NOTES:

NAME..

ADDRESS..

....

MOBILE # (Cell)..

HOME #...

WORK #...

FAX...

EMAIL...

NAME..

ADDRESS..

....

MOBILE # (Cell)..

HOME #...

WORK #...

FAX...

EMAIL...

NAME..

ADDRESS..

....

MOBILE # (Cell)..

HOME #...

WORK #...

FAX...

EMAIL...

NOTES:

NAME...
ADDRESS..
....
MOBILE # (Cell)...
HOME #..
WORK #..
FAX..
EMAIL..

NAME...
ADDRESS..
....
MOBILE # (Cell)...
HOME #..
WORK #..
FAX..
EMAIL..

NAME...
ADDRESS..
....
MOBILE # (Cell)...
HOME #..
WORK #..
FAX..
EMAIL..

NOTES:

NAME..
ADDRESS...
....
MOBILE # (Cell)..
HOME #...
WORK #...
FAX..
EMAIL..

NAME..
ADDRESS...
....
MOBILE # (Cell)..
HOME #...
WORK #...
FAX..
EMAIL..

NAME..
ADDRESS...
....
MOBILE # (Cell)..
HOME #...
WORK #...
FAX..
EMAIL..

NOTES:

NAME..
ADDRESS...
....
MOBILE # (Cell)..
HOME #..
WORK #..
FAX...
EMAIL...

NAME..
ADDRESS...
....
MOBILE # (Cell)..
HOME #..
WORK #..
FAX...
EMAIL...

NAME..
ADDRESS...
....
MOBILE # (Cell)..
HOME #..
WORK #..
FAX...
EMAIL...

NOTES:

NAME...

ADDRESS..

....

MOBILE # (Cell)...

HOME #...

WORK #..

FAX...

EMAIL...

NAME...

ADDRESS..

....

MOBILE # (Cell)...

HOME #...

WORK #..

FAX...

EMAIL...

NAME...

ADDRESS..

....

MOBILE # (Cell)...

HOME #...

WORK #..

FAX...

EMAIL...

NOTES:

.

www.ingramcontent.com/pod-product-compliance
Lightning Source LLC
Chambersburg PA
CBHW060511220326
41598CB00025B/3631